The
POCKET
ALMANAC
of
ESSENTIAL
FACTS

*Everything You Need
To Know*

The
POCKET
ALMANAC
of
ESSENTIAL
FACTS

Everything You Need To Know

GRAMERCY BOOKS
New York • Avenel, New Jersey

Introduction and compilation copyright © 1992 by Outlet Book Company, Inc.
All rights reserved.
First published in 1992 by Gramercy Books
distributed by Outlet Book Company, Inc., a Random House Company,
40 Engelhard Avenue, Avenel, New Jersey 07001

The publisher is not responsible for any action or procedure undertaken by anyone
using first aid information described herein.

Printed and bound in the United States of America

Library of Congress Cataloging-in-Publication Data

Everything you need to know : the handy guide to essential facts.
        p.   cm.
    ISBN 0-517-07389-7
    1. Handbooks, vade-mecums, etc.   I. Gramercy Books (Firm)
AG105.E93 1992
031.02—dc20
                                                                    91-35183
                                                                         CIP

Book design by Clair Moritz

8   7   6   5   4   3   2   1

CONTENTS

INTRODUCTION   7

MEASUREMENTS   9
U.S. System 10
   Length, Area, Cubic Measure, Fluid Measure, Dry
   Measure, Circular Measure, Avoirdupois Weight, Troy
   Weight, Apothecaries' Weight, Apothecaries' Fluid
Measure
Metric (International) System 12
   Length, Area, Cubic Measure, Weight Fluid Measure
Standard Temperature Table 13
Miscellaneous Units of Measure 13
Numbers 15
   Fraction Conversion Table, Prime Number Table, for 1
   to 1000, Large Number Table, Roman Numerals
Conversion Factors 17
Miles to Kilometers, Kilometers to Miles 18
Cooking 19
Temperatures 19
Common Formulas 20
   Circumference and Perimeter, Area, Volume,
   Miscellaneous

TIME   21
Calendars—1992–95 22
Religious Holidays 24
   Christian, Jewish, Muslim
Chinese Calendar 24
Holidays: U.S. and Canada 25
Birthstones 26
Signs of the Zodiac 26
Anniversaries 27
U.S. Time Zones 28
World Time Zones 30
Geologic Time 32

GEOGRAPHY   33
The Fifty States 34
   Post Office Abbreviations, States Capitals, Flowers,
   and Birds
Mileages between U.S. and Canadian Cities 36

Fifty-Seven Nations of the World 38
    Country, Telephone Code, Capital, Currency,
    Maximum and Minimum Temperatures for Major
    Cities
The Solar System 40
    Order of the Planets, Distances from the Sun, Periods
    of Revolution, Rotation Periods, Equatorial Diameters,
    Satellites, Rings
Climate of Major U.S. Cities 42
Weather Symbols 42
Wind-Chill Factors 43
U.S. Telephone Area Codes 44
Toll-Free Telephone Numbers 46

GOVERNMENT 47
U.S. Presidents 48
    Dates, Party, Dates in Office
U.S. Vice Presidents 49
    Dates, Party, Dates in Office
Elected Representatives 50
    U.S. Senators, U.S. Representative, State Senator,
    State Assembly Member, Local Officials

FIRST AID 51
First Aid ABC 52
    To Open the Airway, To Restore Breathing, to Perform
    Artificial Respiration, To Control Bleeding
Burns 54
    To Treat First-Degree Burns, To Treat Second-Degree
    Burns, To Treat Third-Degree Burns
Shock 54
    Symptoms of Shock, To Treat Shock
Choking 55

PERSONAL 57
Information 58
    Identification, Social Security Number, Passport
    Number, Driver's License Number, Bank Account
    Numbers, Safety Deposit Box Number, Insurance
    Policy Numbers, Credit Card Numbers
Emergency Numbers 59
Personal Yellow Pages 60

INTRODUCTION

Did you ever need to know what the currency is in another country, how many kilometers there are in a mile, what time zone another state is in, or how far one city is from another? The answers to these questions and many others can be found in *The Pocket Almanac of Essential Facts*.

Say, for example, that you're invited to an anniversary party for a couple who have been married twenty years. Choosing a present for them is easy when you consult page 27 to learn that the traditional gift for the twentieth wedding anniversary is china.

When you make your grandmother's spaghetti sauce and need to know how many cups there are in a pint, you can find the answer quickly on page 19. And if you have to perform the Heimlich maneuver or treat someone in shock before an ambulance arrives, easy-to-follow instructions are given on pages 53 and 55.

When you are planning a trip, you can consult the calendar on page 22 before calling your travel agent, whose number you've entered in the personal yellow pages on page 60. Just look at the chart on page 42 (or page 38 if you're going abroad) to find the average temperature at your destination so you'll know what clothes to pack. Also of use on your trip might well be the international and U.S. telephone area codes given on pages 44 and 38 and the time zone maps on pages 28 and 30.

Clearly, this little book provides the kind of information frequently needed in ordinary situations. Keep a copy in your briefcase or your purse and one in the glove compartment of your car. You never know when you'll need *The Pocket Almanac of Essential Facts*. It has Everything You Need to Know.

Measurements

U.S. SYSTEM

LENGTH

12 inches	1 foot
3 feet	1 yard
5½ yards	1 rod
40 rods	1 furlong
5,280 feet	1 mile
1,760 yards	1 mile
8 furlongs	1 mile
3 miles	1 league
6,076.11549 feet	1 nautical mile
.8684 nautical miles	1 mile

AREA

144 square inches	1 square foot
9 square feet	1 square yard
30¼ square yards	1 square rod
4,840 square yards	1 acre
43,560 square feet	1 acre
160 square rods	1 acre
640 acres	1 square mile

CUBIC MEASURE

1,728 cubic inches . . .	1 cubic foot
27 cubic feet	1 cubic mile

FLUID MEASURE

3 teaspoons	1 tablespoon
.5 fluid ounce . . .	1 tablespoon
16 tablespoons	1 cup
8 fluid ounces	1 cup
16 fluid ounces	1 pint
2 cups	1 pint
32 fluid ounces	1 quart
2 pints	1 quart
4 cups	1 quart
8 pints	1 gallon
4 quarts	1 gallon

DRY MEASURE
2 pints . . . . . 1 quart
8 quarts . . . . . 1 peck
4 pecks . . . . 1 bushel
32 quarts . . . 1 bushel

CIRCULAR MEASURE
60 seconds . . . . 1 minute
60 minutes . . . . 1 degree
360 degrees . . . . 1 circle
90 degrees . . . . . . right angle
180 degrees . . . . straight angle

AVOIRDUPOIS WEIGHT
27 11/32 grains . . . . 1 dram
16 drams . . . . 1 ounce
16 ounces . . . . 1 pound
256 drams . . . . 1 pound
100 pounds . . . . 1 hundredweight
2,000 pounds . . . . 1 ton
200 hundredweights . . . . 1 ton
112 pounds . . . . 1 gross or long hundredweight
2,240 pounds . . . . 1 gross or long ton

TROY WEIGHT
24 grains . . . . 1 pennyweight
20 pennyweights . . . 1 troy ounce
12 troy ounces . . . . 1 troy pound

APOTHECARIES' WEIGHT
20 grains . . . . 1 scruple
3 scruples . . . . 1 apothecaries' dram
8 apothecaries' drams . . . . 1 apothecaries' ounce
12 apothecaries' ounces . . 1 apothecaries' pound

APOTHECARIES' FLUID MEASURE
60 minims . . . . . . 1 fluid dram
8 fluid drams . . . . 1 fluid ounce
16 fluid ounces . . . . 1 pint
2 pints . . . . 1 quart
4 quarts . . . . 1 gallon
256 fluid drams . . . . . . 1 quart

11

METRIC (INTERNATIONAL) SYSTEM

LENGTH

10 millimeters . . 1 centimeter
10 centimeters . . 1 decimeter
1,000 millimeters . . . 1 meter
100 centimeters . . . . 1 meter
10 meters . . . . . 1 dekameter
1000 meters . . . . 1 kilometer

AREA

100 square millimeters . . . . 1 square centimeter
10,000 centimeters . . . . 1 square meter
10,000 square meters . . . . 1 hectare
1,000,000 square meters . . . 1 square kilometer
100 square hectares . . . . . . 1 square kilometer

CUBIC MEASURE

1,000 cubic millimeters . . 1 cubic centimeter
1,000 cubic centimeters . . 1 cubic decimeter
1,000,000 cubic centimeters . . 1 cubic meter
1,000 cubic decimeters . . . . . 1 cubic meter

WEIGHT

10 milligrams . . . . 1 centigram
10 centigrams . . . . 1 decigram
1,000 milligrams . . . . . 1 gram
100 grams . . . . . . 1 hectogram
1,000 grams . . . . . . 1 kilogram
10 hectograms . . . . 1 kilogram
1,000 kilograms . . 1 metric ton

FLUID MEASURE

10 milliliters . . 1 centileter
10 centileters . . 1 deciliter
1,000 milliliters . . . 1 liter
100 centiliters . . . . 1 liter
10 liters . . . . . 1 dekaliter
1,000 liters . . . . 1 kiloliter

STANDARD TEMPERATURE TABLE

	°Fahrenheit	°Celsius	°Kelvin
Absolute Zero	−459.7	−273.16	0
Freezing Point of Water	32	0	273.16
Normal Human Body Temperature	98.6	37	310.16
Boiling Point of Water	212	100	373.16

MISCELLANEOUS UNITS OF MEASURE

Ampere (Amp): Current produced by an electromotive force of 1 volt through a resistance of 1 ohm

Astronomical Unit (AU): 93,000,000 miles, the mean distance of the earth from the sun

Board Foot: 144 cubic inches (12 inches by 12 inches by 1 inch)

British Thermal Unit (BTU): Amount of heat required to raise the temperature of 1 pound of water by 1 degree Fahrenheit

Carat: 200 milligrams

Cubit: 18 inches

Decibel: The smallest amount of change in loudness detectable by the human ear

Gross: 12 dozen

Hand: 4 inches (10.16 centimeters). Used to measure the height of horses to the withers

Hertz: Wave frequency (cycles) per second

Horsepower: The amount of power required to lift 33,000

pounds 1 foot for 1 minute (equivalent to 1½ times the power of an average horse)

Karat: To measure its purity, any quantity of gold is divided into 24 parts; karats equal how many parts of the 24 are pure (12 karat gold is 50% pure).

Knot: 1 nautical mile per hour, used for ships' speed

Light, speed of: See light-year

Light-year: The distance light travels 1 year in a vacuum— about 5,880,000,000,000 miles (about 186,300 miles per second)

Mach number: The ratio of the speed of an object in a medium, such as air, to the speed of sound in that medium

Magnum: 2 quart bottle

Ohm: Electrical resistance equal to that of a circuit in which a potential change of 1 volt produces a current of 1 ampere

Pi: The ratio of the circumference of a circle to its diameter, or 3.14159+

Pica: ⅙ inch, or 12 points, used in printing

Point: 1/72 inch, used in printing

Ream: 500 sheets of paper

Roentgen: Dosage unit of radiation produced by X-rays

Score: 20 units

Sound, speed of: Approximately 1100 feet per second in 32° Fahrenheit air at sea level. (The speed of sound varies with the temperature and density of the medium.)

Watt: The amount of power used by an electric current of 1 ampere across a potential difference of 1 volt

NUMBERS

FRACTION CONVERSION TABLE[*]

Fraction	Decimal	Percent
1/10	0.1	10
1/8	0.125	12.5
1/6	0.1$\overline{6}$	16.$\overline{6}$
1/5	0.2	20
1/4	0.25	25
3/10	0.3	30
1/3	0.$\overline{3}$	33.$\overline{3}$
3/8	0.375	37.5
1/2	0.5	50
3/5	0.6	60
5/8	0.625	62.5
2/3	0.$\overline{6}$	66.$\overline{6}$
7/10	0.7	70
3/4	0.75	75
4/5	0.8	80
5/6	0.8$\overline{3}$	83.$\overline{3}$
7/8	0.875	87.5
9/10	0.9	90
1/1	1.0	100

[*] Note: A bar above a numeral means that the numeral repeats to infinity. Thus 1/3 = 33.3333333% and so on.

PRIME NUMBER TABLE FOR 1 TO 1,000[*]

	2	3	5	7	11	13	17	19	23
29	31	37	41	43	47	53	59	61	67
71	73	79	83	89	97	101	103	107	109
113	127	131	137	139	149	151	157	163	167
173	179	181	191	193	197	199	211	223	227
229	233	239	241	251	257	263	269	271	277
281	283	293	307	311	313	317	331	337	347
349	353	359	367	373	379	383	389	397	401
409	419	421	431	433	439	443	449	457	461
463	467	479	487	491	499	503	509	521	523
541	547	557	563	569	571	577	587	593	599
601	607	613	617	619	631	641	643	647	653
659	661	673	677	683	691	701	709	719	727
733	739	743	751	757	761	769	773	787	797
809	811	821	823	827	829	839	853	857	859
863	877	881	883	887	907	911	919	929	937
941	947	953	967	971	977	983	991	997	(1009)

[*] Note: A prime number is divisible evenly only by itself or 1.

Number of zeroes after 1	American	British
6	million	million
9	billion	milliard
12	trillion	billion
15	quadrillion	1,000 billion
18	quintillion	trillion
21	sextillion	1,000 trillion
24	septillion	quadrillion
27	octillion	1,000 quadrillion
30	nonillion	quintillion
33	decillion	1,000 quintillion
100	googol	—

ROMAN NUMERALS

Letter	Value	Letter	Value
I	1	L	50
II	2	LX	60
III	3	LXX	70
IV	4	LXXX	80
V	5	XC	90
VI	6	C	100
VII	7	D	500
VIII	8	M	1,000
IX	9	$\overline{V}$	5,000
X	10	$\overline{X}$	10,000
XX	20	$\overline{L}$	50,000
XXX	30	$\overline{C}$	100,000
XL	40	$\overline{D}$	500,000
		$\overline{M}$	1,000,000

Notes:

Repeating a letter repeats its value. Thus MM = 2,000.
Letters of lesser value following an initial letter increase the first letter's value. Thus VI = 6.
Letters of greater value following an initial letter are decreased by the initial letter's value. Thus IV = 4, XC = 90.
Roman numerals are written either in capital or in lowercase letters.

CONVERSION FACTORS

To change	To	Multiply by
acres	hectares	.4047
centimeters	inches	.3937
centimeters	feet	.03281
cubic feet	cubic meters	.0283
cubic meters	cubic feet	35.3145
cubic meters	cubic yards	1.3079
cubic yards	cubic meters	.7646
fathoms	feet	6.0
feet	meters	.3048
gallons (U.S.)	liters	3.7853
grams	grains	15.4324
grams	ounces avdp	.0353
grams	pounds	.002205
hectares	acres	2.4710
inches	millimeters	25.4000
inches	centimeters	2.5400
kilograms	pounds avdp	2.2046
kilometers	miles	.6214
liters	gallons (U.S.)	.2642
liters	pecks	.1135
liters	pints (liquid)	2.1134
liters	quarts (liquid)	1.0567
meters	feet	3.2808
meters	miles	.0006214
meters	yards	1.0936
metric tons	tons (long)	.9842
metric tons	tons (short)	1.1023
miles	kilometers	1.6093
millimeters	inches	.0394
ounces avdp	grams	28.3495
ounces (troy)	ounces (avdp)	1.09714
pecks	liters	8.8096
pints (liquid)	liters	.4732
pounds avdp	kilograms	.4536

To change	To	Multiply by
quarts (liquid)	liters	.9463
rods	meters	5.029
square feet	square meters	.0929
square kilometers	square miles	.3861
square meters	square yards	1.1960
square miles	square kilometers	2.5900
square yards	square meters	.8361
tons (long)	metric tons	1.016
tons (short)	metric tons	.9072
yards	meters	.9144

MILES TO KILOMETERS
KILOMETERS TO MILES

Miles	Kilometers	Kilometers	Miles
1	1.6	1	0.6
2	3.2	2	1.2
3	4.8	3	1.8
4	6.4	4	2.4
5	8.0	5	3.1
6	9.6	6	3.7
7	11.2	7	4.3
8	12.8	8	4.9
9	14.4	9	5.5
10	16.0	10	6.2
20	32.1	20	12.4
30	48.2	30	18.6
40	64.3	40	24.8
50	80.4	50	31.0
60	96.5	60	37.2
70	112.6	70	43.4
80	128.7	80	49.7
90	144.8	90	55.9
100	160.9	100	62.1
1,000	1609	1,000	621

COOKING

1 teaspoon	5 milliliters	100 milliliters	3.4 fluid ounces
1 tablespoon	15 milliliters	240 milliliters	1 cup
1 cup	240 milliliters	1 liter	34 fluid ounces
1 pint	470 milliliters	1 ounce	28 grams
1 quart	.95 liter	1 pound	454 grams
1 gallon	3.8 liters	1 gram	.035 ounce
1 milliliter	1/5 teaspoon	100 grams	3.5 ounces
5 milliliters	1 teaspoon	500 grams	1.10 pounds
15 milliliters	1 tablespoon	1 kilogram	2.205 pounds
34 milliliters	1 fluid ounce		

TEMPERATURES

Degrees Celsius	Degrees Fahrenheit	Degrees Celsius	Degrees Fahrenheit
− 273.1	− 459.6	30	86
− 250	− 418	35	95
− 200	− 328	40	104
− 150	− 238	45	113
− 100	− 148	50	122
− 50	− 58	55	131
− 40	− 40	60	140
− 30	− 22	65	149
− 20	− 4	70	158
− 10	14	75	167
0	32	80	176
5	41	85	185
10	50	90	194
15	59	95	203
20	68	100	212
25	77		

Note: To convert Fahrenheit to Celsius subtract 32 and multiply by 5/9.
To convert Celsius to Fahrenheit, multiply by 9/5 and add 32.

COMMON FORMULAS

CIRCUMFERENCE AND PERIMETER

Circle: πd, in which π is 3.1416 and d = the diameter

Square: 4a, in which a = one side

Rectangle: 2a + 2b, in which a = one side and b = a side perpendicular to a.

AREA

Triangle: $A = \dfrac{ab,}{2}$ in which a = the base and b = the height.

Square: a^2, in which a = one of the sides.

Rectangle: $A = ab$, in which a = the base and b = the height.

Trapezoid: h(a+b), in which h = the height, a = the longer parallel side, and b = the shorter.

Circle: $A = \pi r^2$, in which π is 3.1416 and r = the radius.

VOLUME

Cube: a^3, in which a = one of the edges.

Pyramid: $\dfrac{Ah,}{3}$ in which A = the area of the base and h = the height.

Cylinder: $\pi r^2 h$, in which π is 3.1416, r = the radius of the base, and h = the height.

Cone: $\dfrac{\pi r^2 h,}{3}$ in which π is 3.1416, r = the radius of the base, and h = the height.

Sphere: $\dfrac{4\pi r^3}{3}$ in which π is 3.1416 and r = the radius.

MISCELLANEOUS

Interest: prt, in which p = principal, r = rate of interest, and t = time period.

Time

CALENDARS

1992

January
S	M	T	W	T	F	S
			1	2	3	4
5	6	7	8	9	10	11
12	13	14	15	16	17	18
19	20	21	22	23	24	25
26	27	28	29	30	31	

February
S	M	T	W	T	F	S
						1
2	3	4	5	6	7	8
9	10	11	12	13	14	15
16	17	18	19	20	21	22
23	24	25	26	27	28	29

March
S	M	T	W	T	F	S
1	2	3	4	5	6	7
8	9	10	11	12	13	14
15	16	17	18	19	20	21
22	23	24	25	26	27	28
29	30	31				

April
S	M	T	W	T	F	S
			1	2	3	4
5	6	7	8	9	10	11
12	13	14	15	16	17	18
19	20	21	22	23	24	25
26	27	28	29	30		

May
S	M	T	W	T	F	S
					1	2
3	4	5	6	7	8	9
10	11	12	13	14	15	16
17	18	19	20	21	22	23
24	25	26	27	28	29	30
31						

June
S	M	T	W	T	F	S
	1	2	3	4	5	6
7	8	9	10	11	12	13
14	15	16	17	18	19	20
21	22	23	24	25	26	27
28	29	30				

July
S	M	T	W	T	F	S
			1	2	3	4
5	6	7	8	9	10	11
12	13	14	15	16	17	18
19	20	21	22	23	24	25
26	27	28	29	30	31	

August
S	M	T	W	T	F	S
						1
2	3	4	5	6	7	8
9	10	11	12	13	14	15
16	17	18	19	20	21	22
23	24	25	26	27	28	29
30	31					

September
S	M	T	W	T	F	S
		1	2	3	4	5
6	7	8	9	10	11	12
13	14	15	16	17	18	19
20	21	22	23	24	25	26
27	28	29	30			

October
S	M	T	W	T	F	S
				1	2	3
4	5	6	7	8	9	10
11	12	13	14	15	16	17
18	19	20	21	22	23	24
25	26	27	28	29	30	31

November
S	M	T	W	T	F	S
1	2	3	4	5	6	7
8	9	10	11	12	13	14
15	16	17	18	19	20	21
22	23	24	25	26	27	28
29	30					

December
S	M	T	W	T	F	S
		1	2	3	4	5
6	7	8	9	10	11	12
13	14	15	16	17	18	19
20	21	22	23	24	25	26
27	28	29	30	31		

1993

January
S	M	T	W	T	F	S
					1	2
3	4	5	6	7	8	9
10	11	12	13	14	15	16
17	18	19	20	21	22	23
24	25	26	27	28	29	30
31						

February
S	M	T	W	T	F	S
	1	2	3	4	5	6
7	8	9	10	11	12	13
14	15	16	17	18	19	20
21	22	23	24	25	26	27
28						

March
S	M	T	W	T	F	S
	1	2	3	4	5	6
7	8	9	10	11	12	13
14	15	16	17	18	19	20
21	22	23	24	25	26	27
28	29	30	31			

April
S	M	T	W	T	F	S
				1	2	3
4	5	6	7	8	9	10
11	12	13	14	15	16	17
18	19	20	21	22	23	24
25	26	27	28	29	30	

May
S	M	T	W	T	F	S
						1
2	3	4	5	6	7	8
9	10	11	12	13	14	15
16	17	18	19	20	21	22
23	24	25	26	27	28	29
30	31					

June
S	M	T	W	T	F	S
		1	2	3	4	5
6	7	8	9	10	11	12
13	14	15	16	17	18	19
20	21	22	23	24	25	26
27	28	29	30			

July
S	M	T	W	T	F	S
				1	2	3
4	5	6	7	8	9	10
11	12	13	14	15	16	17
18	19	20	21	22	23	24
25	26	27	28	29	30	31

August
S	M	T	W	T	F	S
1	2	3	4	5	6	7
8	9	10	11	12	13	14
15	16	17	18	19	20	21
22	23	24	25	26	27	28
29	30	31				

September
S	M	T	W	T	F	S
			1	2	3	4
5	6	7	8	9	10	11
12	13	14	15	16	17	18
19	20	21	22	23	24	25
26	27	28	29	30		

October
S	M	T	W	T	F	S
					1	2
3	4	5	6	7	8	9
10	11	12	13	14	15	16
17	18	19	20	21	22	23
24	25	26	27	28	29	30
31						

November
S	M	T	W	T	F	S
	1	2	3	4	5	6
7	8	9	10	11	12	13
14	15	16	17	18	19	20
21	22	23	24	25	26	27
28	29	30				

December
S	M	T	W	T	F	S
			1	2	3	4
5	6	7	8	9	10	11
12	13	14	15	16	17	18
19	20	21	22	23	24	25
26	27	28	29	30	31	

1994

January
S	M	T	W	T	F	S
						1
2	3	4	5	6	7	8
9	10	11	12	13	14	15
16	17	18	19	20	21	22
23	24	25	26	27	28	29
30	31					

February
S	M	T	W	T	F	S
		1	2	3	4	5
6	7	8	9	10	11	12
13	14	15	16	17	18	19
20	21	22	23	24	25	26
27	28					

March
S	M	T	W	T	F	S
		1	2	3	4	5
6	7	8	9	10	11	12
13	14	15	16	17	18	19
20	21	22	23	24	25	26
27	28	29	30	31		

April
S	M	T	W	T	F	S
					1	2
3	4	5	6	7	8	9
10	11	12	13	14	15	16
17	18	19	20	21	22	23
24	25	26	27	28	29	30

May
S	M	T	W	T	F	S
1	2	3	4	5	6	7
8	9	10	11	12	13	14
15	16	17	18	19	20	21
22	23	24	25	26	27	28
29	30	31				

June
S	M	T	W	T	F	S
			1	2	3	4
5	6	7	8	9	10	11
12	13	14	15	16	17	18
19	20	21	22	23	24	25
26	27	28	29	30		

July
S	M	T	W	T	F	S
					1	2
3	4	5	6	7	8	9
10	11	12	13	14	15	16
17	18	19	20	21	22	23
24	25	26	27	28	29	30
31						

August
S	M	T	W	T	F	S
	1	2	3	4	5	6
7	8	9	10	11	12	13
14	15	16	17	18	19	20
21	22	23	24	25	26	27
28	29	30	31			

September
S	M	T	W	T	F	S
				1	2	3
4	5	6	7	8	9	10
11	12	13	14	15	16	17
18	19	20	21	22	23	24
25	26	27	28	29	30	

October
S	M	T	W	T	F	S
						1
2	3	4	5	6	7	8
9	10	11	12	13	14	15
16	17	18	19	20	21	22
23	24	25	26	27	28	29
30	31					

November
S	M	T	W	T	F	S
		1	2	3	4	5
6	7	8	9	10	11	12
13	14	15	16	17	18	19
20	21	22	23	24	25	26
27	28	29	30			

December
S	M	T	W	T	F	S
				1	2	3
4	5	6	7	8	9	10
11	12	13	14	15	16	17
18	19	20	21	22	23	24
25	26	27	28	29	30	31

1995

January
S	M	T	W	T	F	S
1	2	3	4	5	6	7
8	9	10	11	12	13	14
15	16	17	18	19	20	21
22	23	24	25	26	27	28
29	30	31				

February
S	M	T	W	T	F	S
			1	2	3	4
5	6	7	8	9	10	11
12	13	14	15	16	17	18
19	20	21	22	23	24	25
26	27	28				

March
S	M	T	W	T	F	S
			1	2	3	4
5	6	7	8	9	10	11
12	13	14	15	16	17	18
19	20	21	22	23	24	25
26	27	28	29	30	31	

April
S	M	T	W	T	F	S
						1
2	3	4	5	6	7	8
9	10	11	12	13	14	15
16	17	18	19	20	21	22
23	24	25	26	27	28	29
30						

May
S	M	T	W	T	F	S
	1	2	3	4	5	6
7	8	9	10	11	12	13
14	15	16	17	18	19	20
21	22	23	24	25	26	27
28	29	30	31			

June
S	M	T	W	T	F	S
				1	2	3
4	5	6	7	8	9	10
11	12	13	14	15	16	17
18	19	20	21	22	23	24
25	26	27	28	29	30	

July
S	M	T	W	T	F	S
						1
2	3	4	5	6	7	8
9	10	11	12	13	14	15
16	17	18	19	20	21	22
23	24	25	26	27	28	29
30	31					

August
S	M	T	W	T	F	S
		1	2	3	4	5
6	7	8	9	10	11	12
13	14	15	16	17	18	19
20	21	22	23	24	25	26
27	28	29	30	31		

September
S	M	T	W	T	F	S
					1	2
3	4	5	6	7	8	9
10	11	12	13	14	15	16
17	18	19	20	21	22	23
24	25	26	27	28	29	30

October
S	M	T	W	T	F	S
1	2	3	4	5	6	7
8	9	10	11	12	13	14
15	16	17	18	19	20	21
22	23	24	25	26	27	28
29	30	31				

November
S	M	T	W	T	F	S
			1	2	3	4
5	6	7	8	9	10	11
12	13	14	15	16	17	18
19	20	21	22	23	24	25
26	27	28	29	30		

December
S	M	T	W	T	F	S
					1	2
3	4	5	6	7	8	9
10	11	12	13	14	15	16
17	18,	19	20	21	22	23
24	25	26	27	28	29	30
31						

RELIGIOUS HOLIDAYS

CHRISTIAN

Year	Ash Wednesday	Easter Sunday	Pentecost	Trinity Sunday	Advent
1992	Mar. 4	Apr. 19	June 7	June 14	Nov. 29
1993	Feb. 24	Apr. 11	May 30	June 6	Nov. 28
1994	Feb. 16	Apr. 3	May 22	May 29	Nov. 27
1995	Mar. 1	Apr. 16	June 4	June 11	Dec. 3

JEWISH

Year	Rosh Hashanah	Yom Kippur	Sukkoth	Hanukkah	Purim	Pesach
5752 (1991–92)	Sept. 9	Sept. 18	Sept. 23	Dec. 2	Mar. 19	Apr. 18
5753 (1992–93)	Sept. 28	Oct. 7	Oct. 12	Dec. 20	Mar. 7	Apr. 6
5754 (1993–94)	Sept. 16	Sept. 25	Sept. 30	Dec. 9	Feb. 25	Mar. 27
5755 (1994–95)	Sept. 6	Sept. 15	Sept. 20	Nov. 28	Mar. 16	Apr. 15

MUSLIM

Year	New Year's Day, 1 Muharram	1 Ramadan	Id al-Fitr, 1 Shawwal	Id al-Adha, 10 Dhu al-Hijja
1412 (1991-92)	July 12, 1991	Mar. 6, 1992	Apr. 4, 1992	June 11, 1992
1413 (1992-93)	July 1, 1992	Feb. 23, 1993	Mar. 25, 1993	June 1, 1993
1414 (1993-94)	June 20, 1993	Feb. 12, 1994	Mar. 14, 1994	May 21, 1994
1415 (1994-95)	June 9, 1994	Feb. 1, 1995	Mar. 3, 1995	May 10, 1995

CHINESE CALENDAR

Ox	Tiger	Rabbit	Dragon	Snake	Horse
1901	1902	1903	1904	1905	1906
1913	1914	1915	1916	1917	1918
1925	1926	1927	1928	1929	1930
1937	1938	1939	1940	1941	1942
1949	1950	1951	1952	1953	1954
1961	1962	1963	1964	1965	1966
1973	1974	1975	1976	1977	1978
1985	1986	1987	1988	1989	1990

HOLIDAYS: U.S. AND CANADA

	1992[1]	1993	1994	1995
New Year's Day[2]	Jan. 1	Jan. 1	Jan. 1	Jan. 1
Martin Luther King, Jr., Day[2]	Jan. 20	Jan. 18	Jan. 17	Jan. 16
Groundhog Day	Feb. 2	Feb. 2	Feb. 2	Feb. 2
St. Valentine's Day	Feb. 14	Feb. 14	Feb. 14	Feb. 14
Presidents Day[2]	Feb. 17	Feb. 15	Feb. 21	Feb. 20
Mardi Gras	Mar. 3	Feb. 23	Feb. 15	Feb. 28
St. Patrick's Day	Mar. 17	Mar. 17	Mar. 17	Mar. 17
April Fool's Day	Apr. 1	Apr. 1	Apr. 1	Apr. 1
Daylight Savings begins	Apr. 5	Apr. 4	Apr. 3	Apr. 2
Mother's Day	May 10	May 9	May 8	May 14
Armed Forces Day	May 16	May 15	May 21	May 20
Memorial Day[2]	May 25	May 31	May 30	May 29
Father's Day	June 21	June 20	June 19	June 18
Independence Day[2]	July 4	July 4	July 4	July 4
Labor Day[2,3]	Sept. 7	Sept. 6	Sept. 5	Sept. 4
Columbus Day[2]	Oct. 12	Oct. 11	Oct. 10	Oct. 9
Thanksgiving Day (Can.)[3]	Oct. 12	Oct. 11	Oct. 10	Oct. 9
Daylight Saving ends	Oct. 25	Oct. 31	Oct. 30	Oct. 29
Halloween	Oct. 31	Oct. 31	Oct. 31	Oct. 31
Election Day (U.S.)	Nov. 3	Nov. 2	Nov. 8	Nov. 7
Veterans'[2]	Nov. 11	Nov. 11	Nov. 11	Nov. 11
Remembrance Day[3]	Nov. 11	Nov. 11	Nov. 11	Nov. 11
Thanksgiving Day (U.S.)	Nov. 26	Nov. 25	Nov. 24	Nov. 23
Christmas Day[2,3]	Dec. 25	Dec. 25	Dec. 25	Dec. 25
Boxing Day[3]	Dec. 26	Dec. 26	Dec. 26	Dec. 26
New Year's Eve	Dec. 31	Dec. 31	Dec. 31	Dec. 31

Notes: 1. Leap year: February has 29 days. 2. Federal holiday in the United States. 3. Federal holiday in Canada.

Sheep (Goat)	Monkey	Rooster	Dog	Pig	Rat
1907	1908	1909	1910	1911	1912
1919	1920	1921	1922	1923	1924
1931	1932	1933	1934	1935	1936
1943	1944	1945	1946	1947	1948
1955	1956	1957	1958	1959	1960
1967	1968	1969	1970	1971	1972
1979	1980	1981	1982	1983	1984
1991	1992	1993	1994	1995	1996

BIRTHSTONES

Month	Stone	Significance
January	Garnet	Constancy
February	Amethyst	Sincerity
March	Aquamarine	Wisdom
April	Diamond	Innocence
May	Emerald	Love
June	Alexandrite, Pearl	Wealth
July	Ruby	Freedom
August	Peridot	Friendship
September	Sapphire	Truth
October	Tourmaline, Opal	Hope
November	Topaz	Loyalty
December	Turquoise	Success

SIGNS OF THE ZODIAC

Name	Symbol	Period
♈ Aries	The Ram	Mar. 21–Apr. 19
♉ Taurus	The Bull	Apr. 20–May 20
♊ Gemini	The Twins	May 21–June 20
♋ Cancer	The Crab	June 21–July 22
♌ Leo	The Lion	July 23–Aug. 22
♍ Virgo	The Virgin	Aug. 23–Sept. 23
♎ Libra	The Balance	Sept. 24–Oct. 23
♏ Scorpio	The Scorpion	Oct. 24–Nov. 21
♐ Sagittarius	The Archer	Nov. 22–Dec. 21
♑ Capricorn	The Goat	Dec. 22–Jan. 19
♒ Aquarius	The Water Bearer	Jan. 20–Feb. 18
♓ Pisces	The Fish	Feb. 19–Mar. 20

ANNIVERSARIES

Anniversary	Gift	Anniversary	Gift
1st	paper	11th	steel
2nd	cotton, calico, straw	12th	silk, nylon, linen
3rd	leather	13th	lace
4th	flowers, fruit, books, linen, silk	14th	agate, ivory
		15th	glass, crystal
5th	wood	20th	china
6th	sweets, iron	25th	silver
7th	wool, copper, brass, bronze	30th	pearl, personal items ruby
8th	bronze, pottery, rubber	35th	coral, jade
		40th	ruby garnet
9th	pottery, willow, china, glass, crystal	45th	sapphire
		50th	gold
		55th	turquoise, emerald
10th	tin, aluminum	60th	diamond, gold
		75th	diamond, gold

U.S. TIME ZONES

Ontario

Quebec

Newfoundland

New Brunswick

WI

MI

ME

VT NH

NY

MA

CT RI

IL

IN

OH

PA

NJ

KY

WV

MD DE

DC

VA

TN

NC

SC

MS

AL

GA

FL

TIME ZONES OF THE WORLD

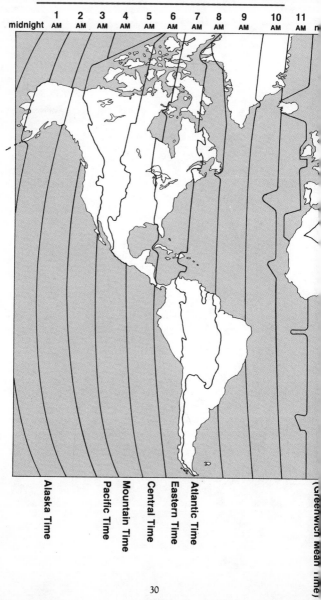

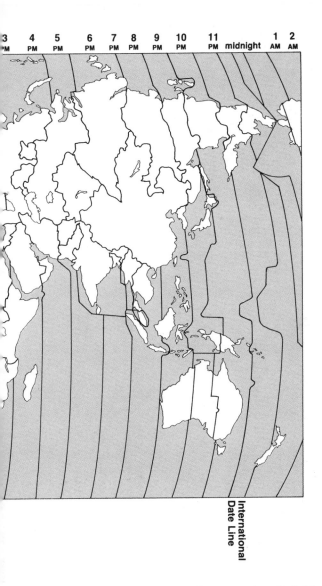

Note: Standard time zones in the former Soviet Union are one hour ahead of the time zones determined by longitude. Daylight Savings Time will advance the time by one hour in countries adopting it in summer.

GEOLOGIC TIME

Era or Eon	Period	Epoch	Animals and Plants	Millions of years ago
Precambrian Time { ARCHEOZOIC			Invertebrates	4,600
PROTEROZOIC			Marine algae	2,500
PALEOZOIC	Cambrian			570
	Ordovician		Fishes, mosses	500
	Silurian			425
	Devonian		Amphibians, vascular plants	395
	Carboniferous		Reptiles, insects, gymnosperms	350
	Permian			290
MESOZOIC	Triassic		Cycads, conifers, ginkoes	235
	Jurassic			190
	Cretaceous		Mammals, birds	130
CENOZOIC	Tertiary	Paleocene	Placental mammals, grasses, grains, flowering plants	65
		Eocene		55
		Oligocene		38
		Miocene		26
		Pliocene		6
	Quaternary	Pleistocene	Humankind	1.8
		Holocene		0.01 (11,000 yrs)

Phanerozoic Time (brackets PALEOZOIC, MESOZOIC, CENOZOIC)

Geography

THE FIFTY STATES

State	Capital	State Flower	State Bird
Alabama (AL)	Montgomery	Camellia	Yellowhammer
Alaska (AK)	Juneau	Forget-me-not	Willow ptarmigan
Arizona (AZ)	Phoenix	Saquaro cactus flower	Cactus wren
Arkansas (AR)	Little Rock	Apple blossom	Mockingbird
California (CA)	Sacramento	Golden poppy	California valley quail
Colorado (CO)	Denver	Rocky Mountain columbine	Lark bunting
Connecticut (CT)	Hartford	Mountain laurel	American robin
Delaware (DE)	Dover	Peach blossom	Blue hen
Florida (FL)	Tallahassee	Orange blossom	Mockingbird
Georgia (GA)	Atlanta	Cherokee rose	Brown thrasher
Hawaii (HI)	Honolulu	Hibiscus	Nene
Idaho (ID)	Boise	Syringia	Mountain bluebird
Illinois (IL)	Springfield	Violet	Cardinal
Indiana (IN)	Indianapolis	Peony	Cardinal
Iowa (IA)	Des Moines	Wild rose	Eastern goldfinch
Kansas (KS)	Topeka	Sunflower	Western meadowlark
Kentucky (KY)	Frankfort	Goldenrod	Kentucky cardinal
Louisiana (LA)	Baton Rouge	Magnolia	Pelican
Maine (ME)	Augusta	White pine cone	Chickadee
Maryland (MD)	Annapolis	Black-eyed susan	Baltimore oriole
Massachusetts (MA)	Boston	Mayflower	Chickadee
Michigan (MI)	Lansing	Apple blossom	Robin
Minnesota (MN)	St. Paul	Snowy lady slipper	Common loon
Mississippi (MS)	Jackson	Magnolia	Mockingbird
Missouri (MO)	Jefferson City	Hawthorn	Bluebird
Montana (MT)	Helena	Bitteroot	Western meadowlark
Nebraska (NE)	Lincoln	Goldenrod	Western meadowlark

State	Capital	State Flower	State Bird
Nevada (NV)	Carson City	Sagebrush	Mountain bluebird
New Hampshire (NH)	Concord	Purple Lilac	Purple finch
New Jersey (NJ)	Trenton	Purple violet	Eastern goldfinch
New Mexico (NM)	Santa Fe	Yucca	Roadrunner
New York (NY)	Albany	Rose	Bluebird
North Carolina (NC)	Raleigh	Dogwood	Cardinal
North Dakota (ND)	Bismark	Wild pairie rose	Western meadowlark
Ohio (OH)	Columbus	Scarlet carnation	Cardinal
Oklahoma (OK)	Oklahoma City	Mistletoe	Scissor-tailed flycatcher
Oregon (OR)	Salem	Oregon grape	Western meadowlark
Pennsylvania (PA)	Harrisburg	Mountain laurel	Ruffed grouse
Rhode Island (RI)	Providence	violet	Rhode Island red
South Carolina (SC)	Columbia	Carolina yellow jessamine	Carolina wren
South Dakota (SD)	Pierre	American pasque-flower	Ring-necked pheasant
Tennessee (TN)	Nashville	Iris	Mockingbird
Texas (TX)	Austin	Bluebonnet	Mockingbird
Utah (UT)	Salt Lake City	Sego lily	Seagull
Vermont (VT)	Montpelier	Red clover	Hermit thrush
Virginia (VA)	Richmond	American dogwood	Cardinal
Washington (WA)	Olympia	Western rhododendron	Willow goldfinch
West Virginia (WV)	Charleston	Rhododendron	Cardinal
Wisconsin (WI)	Madison	Wood violet	Robin
Wyoming (WY)	Cheyenne	Indian paintbrush	Meadowlark

MILEAGES BETWEEN U.S. AND CANADIAN CITIES

All distances in miles

	Albuquerque, NM	Atlanta, GA	Baltimore, MD	Boston, MA	Chicago, IL	Cincinnati, OH	Cleveland, OH	Dallas, TX	Denver, CO	Des Moines, IA	Detroit, MI	Houston, TX	Kansas City, KS
Albuquerque, NM		1394	1890	2192	1290	1376	1580	640	420	996	1540	830	790
Atlanta, GA	1394		671	1070	693	460	684	807	1400	893	728	816	809
Baltimore, MD	1890	671		401	689	492	352	1459	1703	1023	509	1447	1097
Boston, MA	2192	1070	401		973	874	630	1817	1987	1309	697	1914	1454
Chicago, IL	1290	693	689	973		293	341	934	1014	336	273	1083	497
Cincinnati, OH	1376	460	492	874	293		242	941	1167	569	263	1038	588
Cleveland, OH	1580	684	352	630	341	242		1185	1355	677	165	1282	822
Dallas, TX	640	807	1459	1817	934	941	1185		782	702	1186	240	497
Denver, CO	420	1400	1703	1987	1014	1167	1355	782		677	1282	1024	602
Des Moines, IA	996	893	1023	1309	336	569	677	702	677		604	944	211
Detroit, MI	1540	728	509	697	273	263	165	1186	1282	604		1335	749
Houston, TX	830	816	1447	1914	1083	1038	1282	240	1024	944	1335		739
Kansas City, KS	790	809	1097	1454	497	588	822	497	602	211	749	739	
Los Angeles, CA	804	2195	2693	3050	2093	2184	2418	1401	1132	1799	2345	1441	1594
Memphis, TN	1032	367	945	1353	542	477	721	462	1033	606	711	559	457
Miami, FL	2016	665	1144	1540	1358	1124	1301	1307	2044	1557	1345	1214	1468
Minneapolis, MN	1245	1103	1095	1383	410	703	551	954	839	250	683	1196	455
Montreal	2110	1232	560	322	846	818	574	1761	1860	1182	571	1858	1322
New Orleans, LA	1136	494	1136	1534	927	818	1061	496	1280	987	1083	357	819
New York, NY	2002	857	185	214	841	657	505	1605	1849	1171	665	1634	1317
Omaha, NE	718	817	1026	1458	493	622	819	661	559	123	754	903	204
Philadelphia, PA	1920	768	95	302	760	576	424	1524	1769	1090	584	1544	1236
Phoenix, AZ	456	1812	2323	2680	1720	1814	2048	1002	816	1428	1975	1151	1224
St. Louis, MO	1042	560	815	1176	289	336	544	643	854	334	541	792	250
Salt Lake City, UT	612	1902	2116	2403	1429	1642	1770	1239	510	1982	1698	1429	1114
San Francisco, CA	1128	2525	2874	3162	2187	2400	2328	1804	1268	1850	2456	1953	1872
Seattle, WA	1480	2754	2746	3034	2061	2354	2402	2110	1345	1771	2334	2300	1870
Washington, DC	1840	632	37	435	685	490	349	1370	1694	1016	509	1408	1045

Los Angeles, CA	Memphis, TN	Miami, FL	Minneapolis, MN	Montreal	New Orleans, LA	New York, NY	Omaha, NE	Philadelphia, PA	Phoenix, AZ	St. Louis, MO	Salt Lake City, UT	San Francisco, CA	Seattle, WA	Washington, DC
804	1032	2016	1245	2110	1136	2002	718	1920	456	1042	612	1128	1480	1840
2195	367	665	1103	1232	494	857	817	768	1812	560	1902	2525	2754	632
2693	945	1144	1095	560	1136	185	1026	95	2323	815	2116	2874	2746	37
5050	1353	1540	1383	322	1534	214	1458	302	2680	1176	2403	3162	3034	435
2093	542	1358	410	846	927	841	493	760	1720	289	1429	2187	2061	685
2183	477	1124	703	818	818	657	622	576	1814	336	1642	2400	2354	490
2418	721	1301	551	574	1061	505	819	424	2048	544	1770	2328	2402	349
1401	462	1307	954	1761	496	1605	661	1524	1003	643	1239	1804	2110	1370
1132	1033	2044	839	1860	1280	1849	559	1769	816	854	510	1268	1345	1694
1799	606	1557	250	1182	987	1171	123	1090	1428	334	1092	1850	1771	1016
2345	711	1345	683	571	1083	665	754	584	1975	541	1698	2456	2334	509
1551	559	1214	1196	1858	357	1634	903	1544	1151	792	1429	1953	2300	1408
1594	457	1468	455	1322	819	1317	204	1236	1224	250	1114	1872	1870	1045
	1829	2710	1938	2918	1899	2913	1733	2719	396	1846	732	401	1143	2642
1829		1009	838	1297	399	1136	658	1055	1464	292	1532	2155	2329	906
2710	1009		1768	1703	873	1329	1683	1239	2314	1221	2543	3073	3419	1103
1938	838	1768		1256	1239	1251	373	1170	1628	538	1228	1995	1639	1095
2918	1297	1703	1256		1640	386	1833	465	2548	1114	2271	3029	2695	598
1899	399	873	1239	1640		1323	1043	1233	1501	693	1737	2301	2608	1097
2913	1136	1329	1251	386	1323		1315	90	2457	964	2265	3023	2092	223
1733	658	1683	373	1833	1043	1315		1233	1305	459	967	1721	1705	1178
2719	1055	1239	1170	465	1233	90	1233		2462	883	2184	2942	2821	134
396	1464	2314	1628	2548	1501	2457	1305	2462		1476	651	798	1539	2272
1846	292	1221	538	1114	693	964	459	883	1476		1366	2124	2107	798
723	1532	2543	1228	2271	1737	2265	967	2184	651	1366		757	869	2109
401	2155	3073	1995	3029	2301	3023	1721	2942	798	2124	757		825	2867
1143	2329	3419	1639	2695	2608	2902	1705	2821	1539	2107	869	825		2746
2642	906	1103	1095	598	1097	223	1178	134	2272	798	2109	2867	2746	

FIFTY-SEVEN NATIONS
OF THE WORLD

Country and Telephone code	Capital	Currency	City	Climate Jan.	July
Afghanistan (†)	Kabul	afghani	Kabul	18°F	92°F
Australia (61)	Canberra	Australian dollar	Sydney	78	46
Austria (43)	Vienna	schilling	Vienna	49	88
Argentina (54)	Buenos Aires	peso	Buenos Aires	85	42
Bangladesh (880)	Dhaka	taka	Dhaka	56	85
Belgium (32)	Brussels	Belgian franc	Brussels	52	87
Brazil (55)	Brasília	cruzeiro	Rio de Janiero	84	63
Canada (19 + 1†*)	Ottawa	Canadian dollar	Toronto	16	79
Chile (56)	Santiago	peso	Santiago	85	37
China (86)	Beijing	renminbi yuan	Shanghai	32	91
Colombia (57)	Bogotà	peso	Bogota	70	70
Commonwealth of Independent States (7)	Minsk	ruble	Moscow	20	65
Czechoslovakia (42)	Prague	kčs	Prague	25	74
Denmark (45)	Copenhagen	krone	Copenhagen	29	72
Egypt (20)	Cairo	Egyptian pound	Cairo	47	96
France (33)	Paris	franc	Paris	32	76
Germany (49)	Bonn	Deutsche mark	Berlin	26	74
Ghana (233)	Accra	cedi	Accra	87	73
Greece (30)	Athens	drachma	Athens	42	90
Hungary (36)	Budapest	forint	Budapest	26	82
Iceland (354)	Reykjavik	króna	Reykjavik	28	58
India (91)	New Delhi	rupee	Calcutta	55	90
Indonesia (62)	Jakarta	rupiah	Jakarta	74	87
Iran (98)	Teheran	rial	Teheran	27	99
Iraq (964)	Baghdad	dinar	Baghdad	39	110
Ireland (353)	Dublin	Irish pound	Dublin	35	67

Israel (972)	Jerusalem	shekel	Jerusalem	41	87
Italy (39)	Rome	lire	Rome	39	88
Japan (81)	Tokyo	yen	Tokyo	29	83
Kenya (254)	Nairobi	shilling	Nairobi	77	51
Lebanon (†)	Beirut	Lebanese pound	Beirut	51	87
Mexico	Mexico City	peso	Mexico City	42	74
Morocco (212)	Rabat	dirham	Casablanca	24	79
Netherlands (31)	Amsterdam	guilder	Amsterdam	34	69
New Zealand (64)	Wellington	New Zealand dollar	Wellington	69	42
Nigeria (234)	Lagos	naira	Lagos	88	74
Norway (47)	Oslo	Norwegian krone	Oslo	20	73
Pakistan (92)	Islamabad	rupee	Karachi	55	91
Peru (51)	Lima	inti	Lima	82	57
Philippines (63)	Manila	peso	Manila	72	88
Poland (48)	Warsaw	zloti	Warsaw	21	75
Portugal (351)	Lisbon	escudo	Lisbon	46	79
Rep. of Singapore (65)	Singapore	Singapore dollar	Singapore	73	88
Saudi Arabia (966)	Riyadh	Saudi rial	Riyadh	46	107
Senegal (221)	Dakar	CFA franc	Dakar	64	88
South Africa (27)	Cape Town	rand	Cape Town	78	45
South Korea (82)	Seoul	won	Seoul	15	84
Spain (34)	Madrid	peseta	Madrid	33	87
Sri Lanka (94)	Colombo	Sri Lankan rupee	Colombo	72	85
Sweden (46)	Stockholm	Swedish krona	Stockholm	23	70
Switzerland (41)	Bern	Swiss franc	Geneva	29	77
Taiwan (886)	Taipei	New Taiwan dollar	Taipei	53	92
Thailand (66)	Bangkok	baht	Bangkok	67	90
Turkey (90)	Istanbul	Turkish lira	Istanbul	36	81
United Kingdom (44)	London	pound sterling	London	44	73
Vietnam (†)	Hanoi	new dong	Hanoi	58	92
Zaire (†)	Kinshasa	zaire	Kinshasa	87	64

* Dial 011 and the country code for station-to-station international calls. International directory assistance is 1-800-874-4000.
† Cannot be dialed directly from the U.S. or Canada.
†* Outside U.S. only. Canada can be dialed directly from the U.S. by using 1 plus the area code.

THE SOLAR SYSTEM

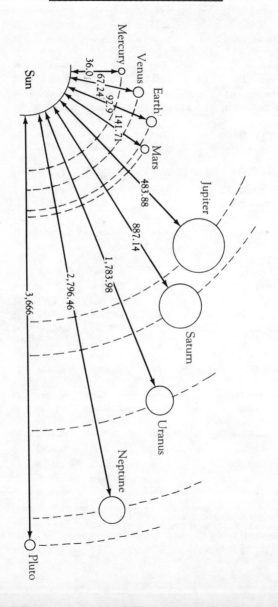

	Mercury	Venus	Earth	Mars	Jupiter
Mean distance from Sun (Millions of miles)	36.0	67.24	92.9	141.71	483.88
Period of revolution	88 days	224.7 days	365.2 days	687 days	11.86 yrs
Rotation period	59 days	243 days retrograde	23 hr 56 min 4 sec	24 hr 37 min	9 hr 55 min 30 sec
Equatorial diameter (Miles)	3,032.4	7,519	7,926.2	4,194	88,736
Atmosphere	Virtually none	Carbon dioxide	Nitrogen oxygen	Carbon dioxide	Hydrogen helium
Satellites	0	0	1	2	16
Rings	0	0	0	0	1

	Saturn	Uranus	Neptune	Pluto
Mean distance from Sun (Millions of miles)	887.14	1,783.98	2,796.46	3,666
Period of revolution	29.46 yrs	84 yrs	165 yrs	248 yrs
Rotation period	10 hr 40 min 24 sec	16.8 hr(?) retrograde	16 hr 11 min(?)	6 days 9 hr 18 mins retrograde
Equatorial diameter (Miles)	74,978	32,193	30,775	1,423 (?)
Atmosphere	Hydrogen helium	Helium hydrogen methane	Hydrogen helium methane	None detected
Satellites	18 +	15	8	1
Rings	1,000 (?)	11	4	?

CLIMATE OF U.S. CITIES

Average high temperatures in degrees Fahrenheit and normal monthly precipitation in inches.

City	Jan.	April	July	October
Baltimore, MD	41° 3.0"	54°	87° 3.9"	57°
Boston, MA	36° 4.0"	49°	82° 2.7"	55°
Chicago, IL	29° 1.6"	49°	83° 3.6"	54°
Cleveland, OH	33° 2.5"	48°	82° 3.4"	53°
Columbus, OH	35° 2.8"		84° 4.0"	
Dallas, TX	54° 1.7"	66°	98° 2.0"	67°
Denver, CO	43° 0.5"	47°	88° 1.9"	52°
Detroit, MI	31° 1.9"	47°	83° 3.1"	52°
El Paso, TX	58° 0.4"	64°	95° 1.6"	64°
Houston, TX	62° 3.2"	69°	94° 4.1"	70°
Indianapolis, IN	34° 2.7"	53°	85° 4.3"	55°

WEATHER SYMBOLS

◎	calm	▲▲▲▲ front, cold	•	rain
○	clear	⌒⌒⌒ warm	∴	rain and snow
◐	cloudy (partly)	▲⌒▲ occluded	∇	shower(s)
		⌒▲⌒ stationary	△	sleet
●	cloudy (completely overcast)	⚲ hurricane	∴	snow
		⚲ tropical storm	⊼	thunderstorm
⌇	drizzle		≡	fog

42

Jacksonville, FL	65°	68°	91°	70°
	1.7″		3.7″	
Los Angeles, CA	67°	60°	84°	66°
	3.7″		—	
Memphis, TN	48°	63°	92°	63°
	4.6″		4.0″	
Milwaukee, WI	26°	45°	80°	51°
	1.7″		3.5″	
New Orleans, LA	62°	69°	91°	69°
	5.0″		6.7″	
New York, NY	38°	52°	85°	58°
	3.2″		3.8″	
Philadelphia, PA	39°	53°	86°	57°
	3.2″		3.9″	
Phoenix, AZ	65°	68°	105°	73°
	0.7″		0.7″	
San Antonio, TX	62°	70°	95°	70°
	1.6″		1.9″	
San Diego, CA	65°	61°	76°	68°
	2.1″		—	
San Francisco, CA	56°	55°	64°	61°
	4.5″		—	
Seattle, WA	45°	49°	75°	52°
	5.9″		0.9″	
Washington, DC	43°	57°	88°	60°
	2.8″		3.9″	

Source: U.S. National Oceanic and Atmospheric Administration, *Comparative Climatic Data for the United States through 1987* (1988)

WIND-CHILL FACTORS

Wind speed (mph)	Thermometer reading (degrees Fahrenheit)											
	35	30	25	20	15	10	5	0	−5	−10	−15	−20
5	33	27	21	19	12	7	0	−5	−10	−15	−21	−26
10	22	16	10	3	−3	−9	−15	−22	−27	−34	−40	−46
15	16	9	2	−5	−11	−18	−25	−31	−38	−45	−51	−58
20	12	4	−3	−10	−17	−24	−31	−39	−46	−53	−60	−67
25	8	1	−7	−15	−22	−29	−36	−44	−51	−59	−66	−74

Note: This chart gives temperature equivalent for combinations of wind speed and temperature.

U.S. TELEPHONE AREA CODES

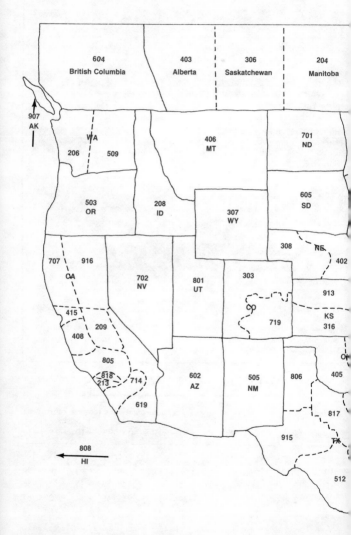

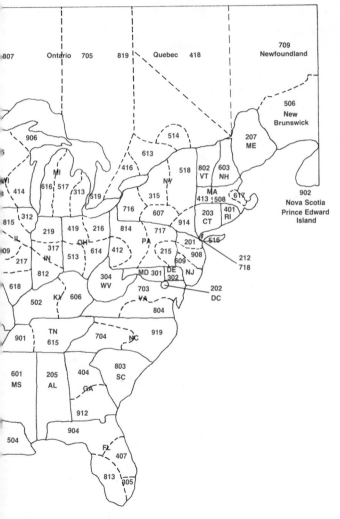

TOLL-FREE TELEPHONE NUMBERS

AIDS Hotline
U.S. Public Health Service
1-800-342-2437
SIDA (Spanish line) 1-800-344-7432
TTY (hearing impaired) 1-800-243-7889

Alcoholism
National Council on Alcoholism Information Line
1-800-622-2255

Alzheimer's Disease
Alzheimer's Disease and Related Disorders Association, Inc.
1-800-621-0379
1-800-572-6037 (Illinois)

Cancer
National Cancer Institute
National Institutes of Health
1-800-638-6694

Civil Rights Hotline
Office of Civil Rights
1-800-368-1019

Drug Abuse
National Institute on Drug Abuse
1-800-662-HELP

National Health Information Center
Department of Health & Human Services
301-565-4167 (Maryland)
1-800-336-4797 (Elsewhere)

Pesticide Hotline
National Pesticide Telecommunications Network
1-800-858-7378

Social Security and Medicare Fraud
Department of Health and Human Services
1-800-368-5779

Toll-Free Information:
1-800-555-1212

Bank and Credit Card Customer Service Numbers

Government

U.S. PRESIDENTS

	Name	Born	Died	Party	In Offi
1.	George Washington	Feb. 22, 1732	Dec. 14, 1799	Fed.	1789–17
2.	John Adams	Oct. 30, 1735	July 4, 1826	Fed.	1797–18
3.	Thomas Jefferson	Apr. 13, 1743	July 4, 1826	Rep.*	1801–18
4.	James Madison	Mar. 16, 1751	June 28, 1836	Rep.*	1809–18
5.	James Monroe	Apr. 28, 1758	July 4, 1831	Rep.*	1817–18
6.	John Quincy Adams	July 11, 1767	Feb. 23, 1848	Rep.*	1825–18
7.	Andrew Jackson	Mar. 15, 1767	June 8, 1845	Dem.	1829–18
8.	Martin Van Buren	Dec. 5, 1782	July 24, 1862	Dem.	1837–18
9.	William Henry Harrison†	Feb. 9, 1773	Apr. 4, 1841	Whig	18
10.	John Tyler	Mar. 29, 1790	Jan. 18, 1862	Whig	1841–18
11.	James Knox Polk	Nov. 2, 1795	June 15, 1849	Dem.	1845–18
12.	Zachary Taylor†	Nov. 24, 1784	July 9, 1850	Whig	1849–18
13.	Millard Fillmore	Jan. 7, 1800	Mar. 8, 1874	Whig	1850–18
14.	Franklin Pierce	Nov. 23, 1804	Oct. 8, 1869	Dem.	1853–18
15.	James Buchanan	Apr. 23, 1791	June 1, 1868	Dem.	1857–18
16.	Abraham Lincoln†	Feb. 12, 1809	Apr. 15, 1865	Rep.‡	1861–18
17.	Andrew Johnson	Dec. 29, 1808	July 31, 1875	Dem.‡	1865–18
18.	Ulysses Simpson Grant	Apr. 27, 1822	July 23, 1885	Rep.	1869–18
19.	Rutherford Birchard Hayes	Oct. 4, 1822	Jan. 17, 1893	Rep.	1877–18
20.	James Abram Garfield†	Nov. 19, 1831	Sept. 19, 1881	Rep.	188
21.	Chester Alan Arthur	Oct. 5, 1830	Nov. 18, 1886	Rep.	1881–188
22.	Grover Cleveland	Mar. 18, 1837	June 24, 1908	Dem.	1885–188
23.	Benjamin Harrison	Aug. 20, 1833	Mar. 13, 1901	Rep.	1889–189
24.	Grover Cleveland	See number 22			1893–189
25.	William McKinley†	Jan. 29, 1843	Sept. 6, 1901	Rep.	1897–190
26.	Theodore Roosevelt	Oct. 27, 1858	Jan. 6, 1919	Rep.	1901–190
27.	William Howard Taft	Sept. 15, 1857	Mar. 8, 1930	Rep.	1909–191
28.	Woodrow Wilson	Dec. 28, 1856	Feb. 3, 1924	Dem.	1913–192
29.	Warren Gamaliel Harding†	Nov. 2, 1865	Aug. 2, 1923	Rep.	1921–192
30.	Calvin Coolidge	July 4, 1872	Jan. 5, 1933	Rep.	1923–192
31.	Herbert Clark Hoover	Aug. 10, 1874	Oct. 20, 1964	Rep.	1929–193
32.	Franklin Delano Roosevelt†	Jan. 30, 1882	Apr. 12, 1945	Dem.	1933–194
33.	Harry S. Truman	May 8, 1884	Dec. 26, 1972	Dem.	1945–195
34.	Dwight David Eisenhower	Oct. 14, 1890	Mar. 28, 1969	Rep.	1953–196
35.	John Fitzgerald Kennedy†	May 29, 1917	Nov. 22, 1963	Dem.	1961–196
36.	Lyndon Baines Johnson	Aug. 27, 1908	Jan. 22, 1973	Dem.	1963–196
37.	Richard Milhous Nixon§	Jan. 9, 1913		Rep.	1969–197
38.	Gerald Rudolph Ford	July 14, 1913		Rep.	1974–197
39.	James Earl Carter, Jr.	Oct. 1, 1924		Dem.	1977–198
40.	Ronald Wilson Reagan	Feb. 6, 1911		Rep.	1981–198
41.	George Herbert Walker Bush	June 12, 1924		Rep.	1989–

* Now the Democratic party † Died in office ‡ Elected on the Union party ticke
§ Resigned * Succeeded to Presidency
‖ Nominated by R. M. Nixon, whom he later succeeded as President
¶ Nominated by G. R. Ford

U.S. VICE PRESIDENTS

	Name	Born	Died	Party	In Office
1.	John Adams	Oct. 30, 1735	July 4, 1826	Fed.	1789–1797
2.	Thomas Jefferson	Apr. 13, 1743	July 4, 1826	Rep.	1797–1801
3.	Aaron Burr	Feb. 6, 1756	Sept. 14, 1836	Rep.	1801–1805
4.	George Clinton†	July 26, 1739	Apr. 20, 1812	Rep.	1805–1812
5.	Elbridge Gerry†	June 17, 1744	Nov. 23, 1814	Rep.	1813–1814
6.	Daniel D. Tompkins	June 21, 1774	June 11, 1825	Rep.*	1817–1825
7.	John C. Calhoun	Mar. 18, 1782	Mar. 31, 1850	Rep.	1825–1832
8.	Martin Van Buren	Dec. 5, 1782	July 24, 1862	Dem.	1833–1837
9.	Richard M. Johnson	Oct. 17, 1781	Nov. 19, 1850	Dem.	1837–1841
10.	John Tyler	Mar. 29, 1790	Jan. 18, 1862	Whig	1841
11.	George M. Dallas	July 10, 1792	Dec. 31, 1864	Dem.	1845–1849
12.	Millard Fillmore*	Jan. 7, 1800	Mar. 8, 1874	Whig	1849–1850
13.	William R. King†	Apr. 7, 1786	Apr.18, 1853	Dem.	1853
14.	John C. Breckinridge	Jan. 21, 1821	May 17, 1875	Dem.	1857–1861
15.	Hannibal Hamlin	Aug. 27, 1809	July 4, 1891	Rep.	1861–1865
16.	Andrew Johnson*	Dec. 29, 1808	July 31, 1875	Dem.‡	1865
17.	Schuyler Colfax	Mar. 23, 1823	Jan. 13, 1885	Rep.	1869–1873
18.	Henry Wilson†	Feb. 16, 1812	Nov. 22, 1875	Rep.	1873–1875
19.	William A. Wheeler	June 30, 1819	June 4, 1887	Rep.	1877–1881
20.	Chester A. Arthur*	Oct. 5, 1830	Nov. 18, 1886	Rep.	1881
21.	Thomas A. Hendricks†	Sept. 7, 1819	Nov. 25, 1885	Dem.	1885
22.	Levi P. Morton	May 16, 1824	May 16, 1920	Rep.	1889–1893
23.	Adlai E. Stevenson	Oct. 23, 1835	June 15, 1914	Dem.	1893–1897
24.	Garret A. Hobart†	June 3, 1844	Nov. 21, 1899	Rep.	1897–1899
25.	Theodore Roosevelt*	Oct. 27, 1858	Jan. 6, 1919	Rep.	1901
26.	Charles W. Fairbanks	May 11, 1852	June 4, 1918	Rep.	1905–1909
27.	James S. Sherman†	Oct. 24, 1855	Oct 30, 1912	Rep.	1909–1912
28.	Thomas R. Marshall	Mar. 14, 1854	June 1, 1925	Dem.	1913–1921
29.	Calvin Coolidge*	July 4, 1872	Jan. 5, 1933	Rep.	1921–1923
30.	Charles G. Dawes	Aug. 27, 1865	Apr. 23, 1951	Rep.	1925–1929
31.	Charles Curtis	Jan. 25, 1860	Feb. 8, 1936	Rep.	1929–1933
32.	John Nance Garner	Nov. 22, 1868	Nov. 7, 1967	Dem.	1933–1941
33.	Henry Agard Wallace	Oct. 7, 1888	Nov. 18, 1965	Dem.	1941–1945
34.	Harry S. Truman*	May 8, 1884	Dec. 26, 1972	Dem.	1945
35.	Alben W. Barkley	Nov. 24, 1877	Apr. 30, 1956	Dem.	1949–1953
36.	Richard M. Nixon	Jan. 9, 1913		Rep.	1953–1961
37.	Lyndon B. Johnson*	Aug. 27, 1908	Jan. 22, 1973	Dem.	1961–1963
38.	Hubert H. Humphrey	May 27, 1911	Jan. 13, 1978	Dem.	1965–1969
39.	Spiro T. Agnew §	Nov. 9, 1918		Rep.	1969–1973
40.	Gerald R. Ford ‖	July 14, 1913		Rep.	1973–1974
41.	Nelson A. Rockefeller¶	July 8, 1908	Jan. 26, 1979	Rep.	1974–1977
42.	Walter F. Mondale	Jan. 5, 1928		Dem.	1977–1981
43.	George H. W. Bush	June 12, 1924		Rep.	1981–1989
44.	J. Danforth Quayle	Feb. 4, 1947		Rep.	1989–

ELECTED REPRESENTATIVES

U.S. Senators

U.S. Congress
Washington, D.C. 20515
phone _____
Home address _____
phone _____

U.S. Congress
Washington D.C. 20515
phone _____
Home address _____
phone _____

U.S. Representative

U.S. Congress
Washington D.C. 20515
phone _____
Home address _____
phone _____

State Senator

Capital address _____
_____
phone _____
Home address _____
phone _____

State Assembly Member

Capital address _____
_____
phone _____
Home address _____
phone _____

Local officials _____
_____
_____
_____

First Aid

First Aid ABC

These are the principles of first aid when serious injury has occurred;

- • A—Open the Airway
- • B—Check Breathing (restore if necessary)
- • C—Control Bleeding

To Open the Airway

- • Use your fingers to remove anything obstructing the mouth and throat.

To Restore Breathing

- • Use artificial respiration (mouth-to-mouth breathing) if the victim's breathing movements have stopped or the fingernails, lips, and tongue are blue. This may happen in cases of electric shock, drowning, or smoke inhalation.

  In the case of a heart attack, a *qualified* person should administer cardiopulmonary resuscitation (CPR), which includes artificial respiration and heart compression by means of rhythmic pressure on the breastbone. CPR must be administered *only* by someone properly trained in the technique. Classes are available through the American Heart Association and the American Red Cross.

To Perform Artificial Respiration:

- • For adults: Place the victim lying flat and face up. Lift the chin and tilt the head back. If necessary, pull the chin up by placing your fingers behind the lower jaw and push forward.

  Take a deep breath and place your mouth over the victim's mouth, taking care to make a leakproof seal.

  Pinch the victim's nostrils closed.

  Blow into the victim's mouth until the chest rises.

  Allow the victim to exhale.

- • Or, take a deep breath and seal your mouth over the victim's nose, holding the mouth closed with your hand.

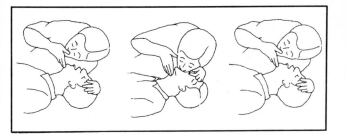

Blow into the victim's nose until you see the chest rise. Allow the victim to exhale.

Repeat twelve times per minute until medical help arrives.

- For infants and children: Place your mouth over the victim's nose and mouth. Blow into the nose and mouth until you see the child's chest rise.
  Allow the child to exhale.

Repeat twenty to thirty times per minute, until help arrives.

To Control Bleeding

Controlling bleeding is almost always very simple: Apply direct pressure to the open wound. This will permit normal blood clotting to occur.

You may be upset by the appearance of the wound and the emotional state of the victim. Remember that a small amount of blood can appear to be a great deal. It is important to keep calm.

- To apply direct pressure, place the cleanest material available (or, if no clean material is available, use your bare hand) against the bleeding point and press firmly with your hand until a cover bandage is applied. When the bandage is applied, it should supply enough pressure to stop the bleeding. Do not remove the bandage until the victim is examined by a physician.

  If the victim continues to bleed after the bandage has been put on, use your hand to put more pressure on the wound over the bandage, or apply a second bandage over the first. Do not remove the original dressing.

Burns

Burns are classified in order of increasing severity, and first aid is different for each.

To Treat First-Degree Burns

- Symptoms: reddened skin.
- First aid: Immerse in cold water until pain stops.

To Treat Second-Degree Burns

- Symptoms: reddened skin and blisters.
- First aid: Remove loose clothing and cover area with several layers of damp, cold dressings. To relieve pain, if possible, immerse the affected area in cold water.

To Treat Third-Degree Burns

- Symptoms: skin destroyed, tissue damage, charring.
- First aid: Remove loose clothing (but do not try to remove clothing that has adhered to wound); cover area with several layers of damp, cold dressings to relieve pain and stop burning action. Treat victim for shock.

Shock

Shock is a collection of symptoms that results from a decrease in the volume of blood circulating through the body and from the body's efforts to compensate for this decrease. Usually it occurs as a consequence of an accident or injury. It can be fatal.

Symptoms of Shock

Early signs of shock are:

- Pale skin
- Rapid pulse
- Cold arms and hands, legs and feet
- Thirst
- Mouth dryness

Followed by:

- Faintness, disorientation, or inexplicable restlessness
- Weak pulse
- Cold sweating and clammy skin
- Decreased urinary output

Followed by:

- Rapid and weak or "thready" pulse, or unobtainable pulse
- Irregular gasping respiration
- Dilated pupils that are slow to respond to light
- Mental confusion
- Eventually, coma and death

To Treat Shock

If the victim is conscious and assuming there has been no injury to the spine or neck, place the victim on a flat surface with the legs raised six to eight inches.

If the victim is unconscious, place him on his side or stomach, with the head turned to the side to prevent choking.

If the spine or neck may be injured, do not attempt to move the victim.

Follow the following procedures:

- Maintain body heat.
- Remove any wet clothing.
- Give warm liquids or foods, or use a warm sleeping bag, or another person to supply external heat. (Do not try to give food or liquids if victim is not conscious.)

CHOKING

When a person's airway is completely obstructed he is unable to speak, breathe, or cough. He will probably clutch the neck in the universal sign of choking. Death can result if action is not taken immediately.

- If the victim's airway is only partially obstructed, encourage coughing.
- If breathing is completely obstructed, stand behind the victim and place your arms around his waist.

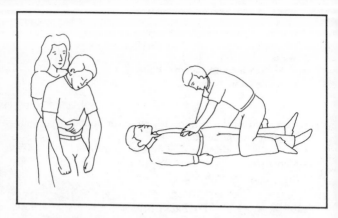

- Position the thumb side of one of your fists against the middle of the victim's abdomen above the navel and below the breastbone.
- Grasp your fist with your other hand.
- In a sharp inward and upward thrust, pull your fist into the victim's abdomen.
- Repeat if necessary.

- If the victim is lying down, turn him or her face up, sit astride the hips, place one of your hands atop the other above the navel and below the breastbone, and push down sharply. Repeat if necessary.

Note: Information in this section was drawn from *First Aid Book*, U.S. Department of Labor, Mine Safety and Health Administration, reprinted 1991, and from *Survival*, U.S. Department of the Army, 1986.
The publisher is not, however, responsible for any action or procedure undertaken by anyone using the first aid information described herein.

Personal Information

Name _____

Address _____

_____

Phone (work) _____

(home) _____

Social Security Number _____

Passport Number _____

Driver's License Number _____

Bank Account Numbers _____

Safety Deposit Box Number _____

Insurance Policy Numbers _____

Blue Cross/Blue Shield Group _____

Major Medical Group _____

Automobile Insurance _____

Home Owner's _____

Life Insurance _____

Other _____

Credit Card Numbers _____

Mastercard _____

Visa _____

American Express _____

Diner's Club _____

Other _____

_____

_____

_____

_____

_____

_____

_____

_____

EMERGENCY NUMBERS

Ambulance _____

Police _____

Fire Department _____

Accountant _____

Appliance Repairs _____

Attorney _____

Automobile Repairs _____

Baby-sitters _____

_____

Dentist _____

Doctors _____

_____

_____

_____

_____

_____

_____

_____

_____

_____

_____

_____

_____

_____

_____

_____

_____

_____

_____

_____

_____

_____

_____

YELLOW PAGES

Dry Cleaner _____

Library _____

Plumber _____

Police Precinct _____

Post Office _____

School _____

Supermarket _____

Travel Agent _____

Veterinarian _____

Video Store _____

Other _____

_____

_____

_____

_____

_____

_____

_____

_____

_____

_____

_____

_____

_____

_____

_____

_____

_____

_____